Hello, I'm Alan! Welcome to my brain-boggling, code-cracking, number-crunching puzzle book!

ALL ABOUT ALAN

Alan Turing was born in London in 1912. He was a mathematical genius whose ideas helped develop modern computing.

During World War II, Alan played an important role at Bletchley Park in the UK. He helped design a machine called the "Bombe." This was used to decode messages from the German military.

Alan Turing's code-breaking skills helped the Allies shorten the war and saved many lives.

THE TURING TRUST

When you buy this book, you are supporting The Turing Trust. This is a charity, set up by Alan's family, in his memory.

The Turing Trust works with disadvantaged communities in Africa to give people access to computers.

Chip and dip

Work out the number pattern for each tortilla chip and dip to find out what numbers are missing on chips C and D.

A: 6 5 3 1

C: 8 7 6 ?

D: 4 ? 4 6

B: 3 6 5 4

Alan Turing's Challenge

If GUACAMOLE = 7.21.1.3.1.13.15.12.5 then what would 19.1.12.19.1 be on a menu?

Leap right in!

Which number should replace the question mark
on the leaf in this pattern?

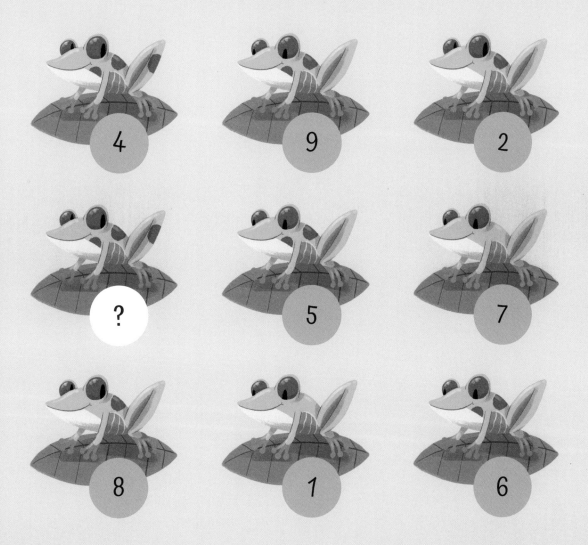

It's Fry-day

How about hash browns for dinner? You have three hash browns to cook, and a tiny frying pan that can only fit two at a time. It takes four minutes to cook one piece (two minutes per side).

How quickly can you cook all three pieces?

Alan Turing's Challenge

How long would it take if you have five pieces to cook in the same pan?

Quick on the draw

Without placing the crayons diagonally, how can you divide this square into two equal parts, by adding just three crayons?

Nice as pie

Which of the pieces of pie should go into each gap?

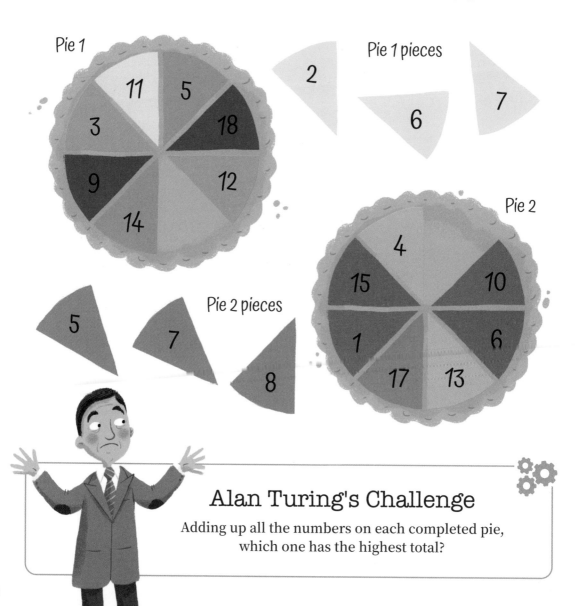

Pie 1

11 5
3   18
9   12
14

Pie 1 pieces

2 6 7

Pie 2 pieces

5 7 8

Pie 2

4
15   10
1   6
17   13

Alan Turing's Challenge

Adding up all the numbers on each completed pie,
which one has the highest total?

Catch me if you can

Two robbers have raided the city bank! Find two routes—one for each robber—from the bank in the middle to the exit at the top.

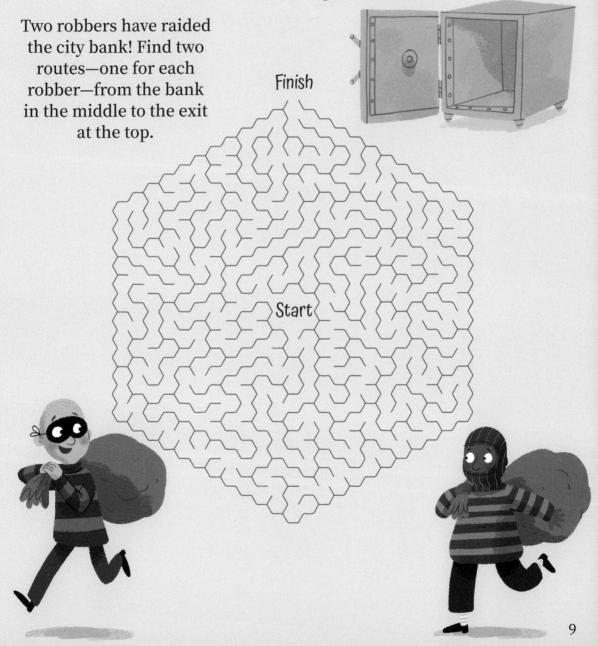

Finish

Start

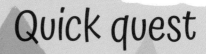

Quick quest

This questing quartet needs to cross a dangerous bridge to reach the ancient treasure. Check the rules below to work out if they can all get across in 15 minutes or less.

The staff will keep them safe while they cross the crumbling bridge, but its magic is only powerful enough to protect two people at any time. Anyone can carry the staff, but they cannot throw it.

Elf Eleanor is fast, and can cross in 1 minute.

Dashing Dwain crosses in 2 minutes.

Dwarf Dullun takes 5 minutes to cross.

Wizard Will needs 8 minutes to get across.

Cube counter

Help the robot work out how many cubes are in this set of blocks.
Each block is supported underneath, with no spaces.

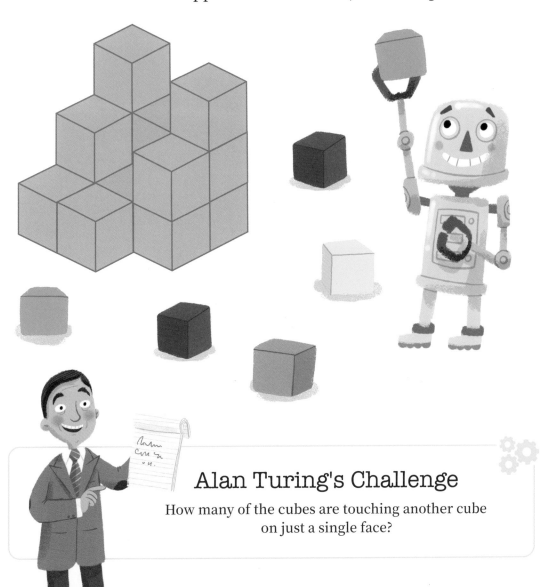

Alan Turing's Challenge

How many of the cubes are touching another cube
on just a single face?

Sticky situation

This sticker album is a bit of a mess. Can you work out which was the first sticker to be stuck on the page?

Alan Turing's Challenge

Which two stickers are not overlapped by any others?

Desert dilemma

There's a fortune to be won if you're smart enough.

A rich camel owner plans to share his fortune.

He gives his son and daughter a camel each and tells them they must compete in a race.

The owner of whichever camel crosses the finish line LAST will win the father's fortune.

The brother and sister set off on their own camels, and ride through the desert for days to avoid crossing the line first.

They seek the help of a wise woman.

When they hear what she has to say, the brother and sister hurry to the camels and race to the finish line.

What did the wise woman say?

Class act

Fourteen of the kids in a class are girls. Eight in the class wear blue shirts. Two who are not girls do not wear a blue shirt. If five of the kids in class are girls who wear blue shirts, how many kids are in the class?

Detective work

You'll need your super sleuth skills to work out this problem. Hint: Add the two paired numbers first.

If 4,7 = 33

And 3,6 = 27

And 5,8 = 39

Then 2,5 = ?

Alan Turing's Challenge

What pair of numbers would give you 45?

Pocket money spend

Six friends have been shopping and spent almost all their pocket money. Put the friends in order from who has the most money left to the one with the least.

Bo has more than Amy but less than Clio.

Dale has more than Clio.

Eric has less than Amy and more than Freya.

Parking puzzle

What numbers belong in the blank
squares in the parking spaces?

Look at the first
example to work it out.

Alan Turing's Challenge

If A = 1, B = 2 and so on, work out the name of the place
where you can find one of the widest roads in the world.
20.5.24.1.19

Pressing matter

Which buttons should the professor press on her computer screen?

Look at the first two patterns of buttons for clues, then shade in the buttons to be pressed in the last square.

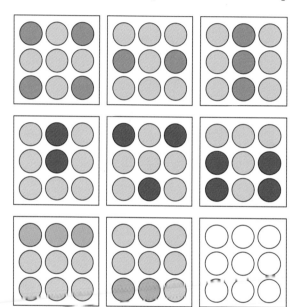

Alan Turing's Challenge

In how many different positions could you place three buttons in a straight line on a 3 x 3 square, above?

Super challenge

Are you super-genius enough to fill in the missing numbers in this grid?

Every hexagon should be made up of six triangles that add up to 27, only using numbers from 1 to 8.

No number can be used more than once within each hexagon.

Red alert

There's trouble at Launch Control. Fill in the missing numbers to fix the problem.

Add two adjacent numbers to find the number that goes directly above them. What is the value of the flashing button?

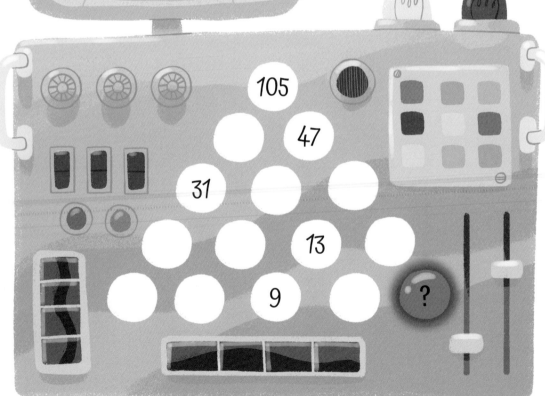

105

47

31

13

9

?

Road trip

The Brownlee family headed out on a road trip to the coast.

They left early to avoid the busy traffic, and drove at 60 km/hour. On their way home, they were held up by traffic jams, and only drove at 30 km/hour.

What was their average speed over the whole journey?

Work of art

How many triangles
can you count
altogether in this
glass pyramid?

Letter delivery

Help the postal worker work out which letter belongs on the blank envelope.

A   C   E

F   H   J

?   M   O

Alan Turing's Challenge

Look at the puzzle instructions carefully, then work out the next three letters in this sequence: HTPWWO __ __ __ .

Put a sock in it

Hugo is getting dressed in the dark so he doesn't wake his little brother in the bed next to him. He needs your help ...

Hugo only wears red striped, red spotted, or plain red socks. He has two pairs of each. How many socks must he take out of the drawer to be sure of having a matching pair when he puts them on in the bathroom?

Team leaders

Put crosses in the grids to mark who captained each team, and in what position they finished.

	Red Captain	Yellow Captain	Green Captain	Blue Captain
Andy				
Chun				
Frieda				
Joe				

	1st	2nd	3rd	4th

1st				
2nd				
3rd				
4th				

Chun's team did not finish fourth.

Andy was red captain and did not finish last.

The blue team came third with Joe as captain.

The team that won wore yellow.

Alan Turing's Challenge

Each team scored 50% more than the team behind it. If the team in fourth position scored 8 points, what did the lead team score?

Prize pups

Work out how much each pup scored in the Doggy Awards. Use the answers to complete the calculation, below.

Diamond robbery

Each side of this diamond-shaped grid is made up of three squares that touch at the corners. The decimal numbers in each diagonal line of three squares add up to the number on the jewel in the middle, 14. What are the missing numbers?

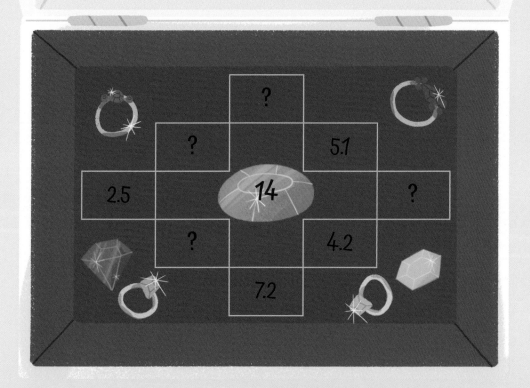

It's a wrap!

A school is recycling wrappers to claim clean-up medals. If a class collected 120 wrappers, how many medals could they claim altogether?

MEDAL REWARD

Receive one point for every eight wrappers you return.

Redeem five points for a medal.

Rainy day games

Which group of four dots on this board game is different from the others?

A

B

C

D

Alan Turing's Challenge

Replace the letters to find another rainy day game, using the code B = A, C = B and so on.

TOBLFT BOE MBEEFST

Get technical

Use robot logic to fill in the missing numbers on this grid. You must only use the numbers from 1 to 9, and follow these rules:

The total of each run of white squares, going across or down, must match the total at the start of that run.

A number cannot repeat within a run.

	16	7		
10			18	
16				5
	7	2		
		13		4

Alan Turing's Challenge

Why would the number below be incorrect if any digits switched position?

8,549,176,320

Full of fruit

Pedro is mixing smoothies with different ingredients for his Spanish friends. Follow the recipe to answer the question at the end.

He pours 100 ml of orange juice into one glass.

He pours 100 ml of pineapple juice into another glass.

Then he takes out exactly one quarter of pineapple juice and tips it into the glass containing orange juice. He mixes it thoroughly.

Then he takes out one quarter of this new mixture and pours it back into the glass containing pineapple juice.

Which glass should Pedro pick if he wants a drink with more orange juice?

Splat attack!

Where did the seven paint splats hit? Each number in the grid shows how many splats touch the number's square (up, down, across or diagonally). Mark where the splats go.

			2	
	4			
2		0		1
1		1		1

Four next door

Can you find the block of four houses on the right in the plan?

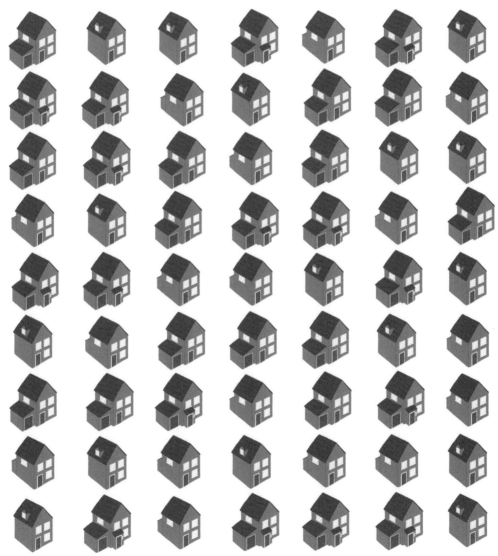

33

Final score

Danny wants to watch the Cup Final, but he won't be home in time for the start so will watch a recording. When should he switch on the TV to avoid seeing the final score?

Kick-off is at 3pm.

The game lasts 90 minutes, with 15 minutes at half-time.

There may be injury time of up to 10 minutes.

If it's a draw, it will go to extra time. The players will rest for 20 minutes, followed by 30 minutes of play.

If it's still a draw after that, there will be a penalty shoot-out. This could add another 20 minutes.

What is the EARLIEST time he can switch on and be sure that he won't spoil the surprise?

Alan Turing's Challenge

If ITALY = LWDOB, BRAZIL = EUDCLO, and GERMANY = JHUPDQB, which World Cup-winning nation is this?
DUJHQWLQD

34

Marble muddle

Each different marble is represented by a letter. Suki has won the marbles D and E in a game. Work out which they are from the groups next to her.

AD

BD

CE

BCD

School run

Which car reaches the school by making the fewest right-hand turns on the way?

The red car has to call at the store first.

The yellow car is late, so it avoids the roadworks and the traffic signals.

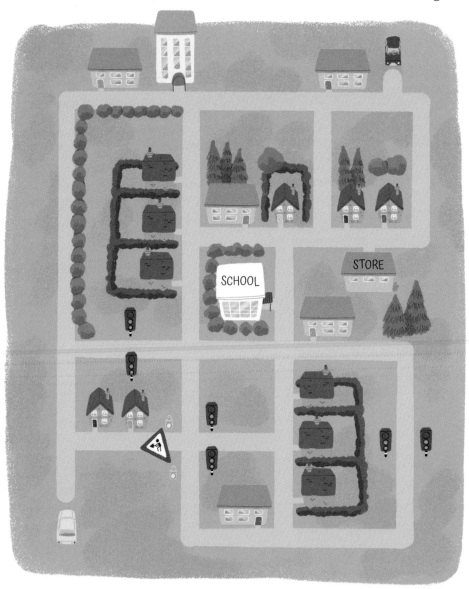

36

Peak performance

What are the missing numbers? The answer is different for each pattern.

Toadstool trail

Where should the 5 toadstools appear on the grid?

Each row, column, and outlined shape has one toadstool. The toadstools cannot be in squares next to each other, even diagonally. One has been done for you.

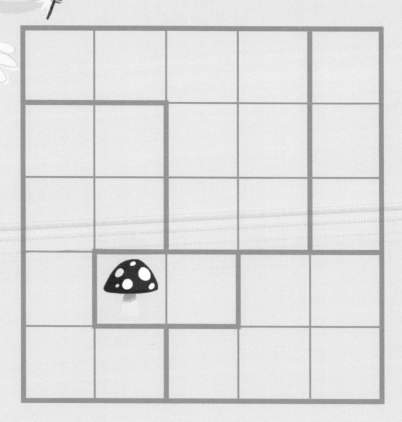

The big read

A bookseller takes delivery of a huge box of books and puts them all on display. She has to divide them several times before she's happy with the outcome.

First, she displays equal amounts on two tables, but has one book left over.

She divides them across three tables, but still has one left over.

The same happens with four tables, and six tables. There's always just one odd book left.

Finally, she displays them across seven tables and has an equal number on each table.

How many books were in the box?

Is the answer
151, 201, or 301?

Alan Turing's Challenge

Why can't you use a bookmark to mark your place between pages 13 and 14 in a book?

Tomb tiles

Archaeologists have uncovered a series of ancient numbered tiles. They all have something in common. What number should be on the blank tile at the bottom?

Alan Turing's Challenge

If A = 26, B = 25 and so on, which country are the archaeologists in?

20.6.26.7.22.14.26.15.26

Game on

Use the clues to work out which sports the kids play.

Ben plays a game that begins with the letter B.

Enrique needs a bat to play his sport.

Camille's sport involves going in the water.

	Basketball	Baseball	Volleyball	Water Polo
Ben				
Camille				
Delany				
Enrique				

Waterworks

The outlined shapes in the grid are containers that can be filled with water. Follow the rules to fill them in, shading the squares blue.

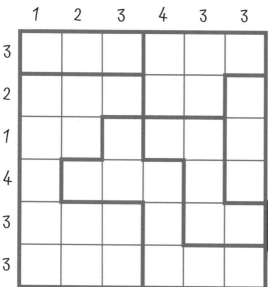

A container can be empty, part-filled, or completely full.

Containers must have the same level of water across the width of the container, and all containers must be filled from the bottom.

The numbers on the top and left of the grid show how many squares are filled in each row or column.

Alan Turing's Challenge

Are more or less than half of the squares filled with water?

Stolen treasure

The pirate captain wants to know who has stolen his booty. He asks his four shipmates, and gets a different reply from each:

Bosun: It wasn't the Navigator. It wasn't the First Mate.

Navigator: It wasn't the First Mate. It was the Bosun.

Cook: It wasn't the Bosun. It was the First Mate.

First Mate: It was the Navigator. Actually, it was the Bosun.

Each one of them uttered one true statement and one false statement.

Who stole the treasure?

Hint: if a pirate accuses two people of being the thief then one must be guilty and one must be innocent. That's also true if a pirate says neither is the thief!

Raccoon rascal

The rascally raccoon has taken a number from the last flowerpot. Which of his numbers will correctly fill the space?

Cyber crime

Can you hunt down the computer viruses before the laptop shuts down? Spot these strings of characters in the code.

sgh12pW

rs9sny

oysw8

Aldsfjiob33dflaoyWlopusdSOUS9723
Aoisdn90Ushg12Pw78d43posynbWO
opus39bmskh70wndb12rs9snyUsgh16
Loysw82nfvts973dtsUIS029souUSso9
19sweiUT49nsoDET031snse87&sidP9
dus8%7wd02HDsienUsg238pWs29fn
8sifAI62ndhHH3r9tisl89^3120bsoeOF
$sad93Usgh12pW11sbeuBE05*esW5
Pwdb06NBwohgy773£sldi98PPdh56
2&ijWEn85idBRose&£lsib3574iiwi8E

Alan Turing's Challenge

How many times does the sequence '12' appear?

A trip to the north

Peter visited Iceland for work.

Peter took a taxi from the airport which cost 18,000kr.

He caught 3 buses each costing 470kr.

He spent three nights in a hotel. Each night cost the same as half his taxi fare.

He bought a tourist pass for 9,000kr but had to pay extra for the Blue Lagoon. The entry for that was a quarter the amount of the tourist pass.

He budgeted 30,000kr for food and drink but only spent 80% of it.

How much did Peter spend on his trip?

Alan Turing's Challenge

Iceland has coins worth 1, 5, 10, 50 and 100 and banknotes worth 500, 1,000, 2,000, 5,000 and 10,000. What is the smallest number of notes and coins you can use to pay exactly 1,425kr?

Black and white

Fill each empty square with a circle, so that each row and column has an equal number of white and black circles. No row and column has the same order, and there cannot be more than two black or two white together in a row or column.

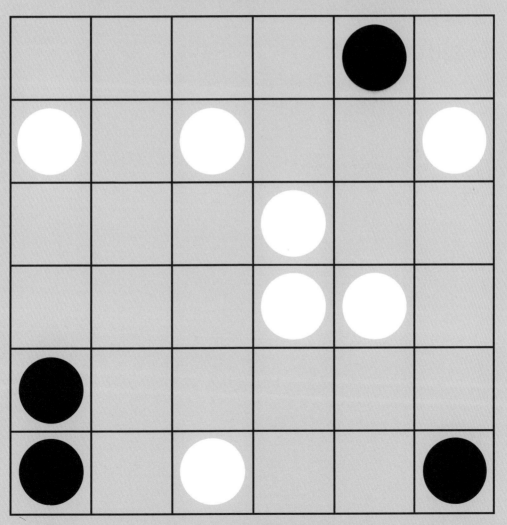

Monster meal

Ready for a monster feast? Draw lines following the dots to divide this square room plan into rectangular tables for each group of monsters.

Each table contains only one number. The number equals the number of squares that make up the table.

Enter the airlock

The astronaut needs to re-enter her spacecraft through the airlock. What single-digit number does she need to punch in to open the outer door (A) and the inner door (B)?

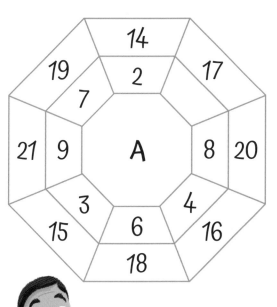

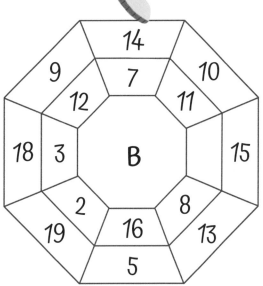

Alan Turing's Challenge

When she left the spacecraft, the astronaut caught sight of an onboard clock. Its hands showed a quarter to five but she was looking at a reflected image. What time was it, really?

Dividing donuts

Caitlyn and Calvin work at a bakery. One day, Caitlyn sets Calvin a riddle:

We need two boxes of donuts to deliver to Adam and Belinda.

If you move one donut from Belinda's box to Adam's then Adam will receive twice as many donuts as Belinda.

If you move one donut from Adam's box to Belinda's, both boxes will contain the same number.

How many donuts has Caitlyn put in each box?

Hint: There are fewer than 10 donuts in each box.

Unique unicorn

Can you find the only unicorn in the magical kingdom that is not part of a pair?

Alan Turing's Challenge

Which are there more of: unicorns with a green body or unicorns with a green mane?

Lily leap

Lead the frog over the lily pads to the finish. You must follow the order pink, green, blue, purple each time. Move up, down, left, or right, but not diagonally.

Start

Finish

Hop and skip

Follow the hopscotch patterns from the bottom to the top.

Starting with the bottom number, can you work out the pattern of squares and triangles that ends with the number in the circle?

What number is missing from the third circle?

10   5   ?

9   2   1

2   3   3

3   5   5

6   9   5

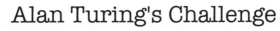

Alan Turing's Challenge

Using only addition, how can you make 1,000 from eight eights?

Up in arms

Complete the shield patterns. Shade them in following the instructions.

25% are divided into quarters.

40% of the total number are divided in half down the middle.

The remainder have no division, but 4 of them have a circle in the middle.

60% of the total number have white on one side.

25% have red on one side.

100% of the quarter patterns are blue and yellow.

50% of the circles are yellow. The rest are black.

How many shields have no pattern at all?

Flying high

Wonder Wing is a factory for making parts for planes.

They made 28 wings, 13 engines, and 22 tail fins each week for the past five weeks.

They plan to double this number for the next six weeks.

How many plane parts will they make in total over the eleven weeks?

Alan Turing's Challenge

If they have three weeks, not six, to double this number, how many tail fins can they make?

Egg hunt

Casey's searching for chocolate eggs. How many will he collect on the route out the maze without retracing his path? Numbers show how many eggs are at each stop.

Finish

4

5

Start

4

7

Birthday drive

Florence and Emma want to buy a driving experience for their dad's birthday. Which deal gives the cheapest rate per hour?

Three 10-minute laps in the yellow sports car, at $26 dollars per lap.

30 minutes in a monster truck, at $150 per hour.

Three hours off-roading in the red jeep for $600, but with a 20%-off discount code.

Sushi challenge

Where should the five sushi rolls appear on the grid? They cannot be next to each other (not even diagonally). One sushi roll goes in each row, column, and outlined shape.

Alan Turing's Challenge

Which of these is NOT an anagram of NIGIRI (sushi with rice and a topping)?

GRINII RINGII RINIGI NIIRGII GINIIR

Feeling crabby

How many crabs are holding a green triangle?
And how many are holding a red square?

Alien encounter

Work out where the aliens are lurking in this grid.

Each number shows how many aliens are touching that square, up, down, or diagonally. Add a cross to show where each goes. There are eight alien squares to find.

2				2
	3	5		
3				
				1
	2	1	1	0

Sheep search

It's time for shearing. Can you find these number sequences in the rows of sheep?

Look for them across, from left to right only.

38	66	84	437	893
895	5782		7596	8575

Sheep rows (numbers on each sheep, left to right):

Row 1: 2 7 3 5 8 9 5
Row 2: 9 5 9 8 4 7 3
Row 3: 4 8 5 7 5 9 6
Row 4: 4 3 7 6 6 0 3
Row 5: 7 4 5 8 9 3 6
Row 6: 9 4 3 8 5 4 3
Row 7: 8 5 7 8 2 4 2

Alan Turing's Challenge

Can you also find the sequence of numbers that is the answer to 11 x 22?

61

Fish feeding

Each of the shaped containers (made of 2 or more squares) can be filled with fish food. Follow the rules to fill them in correctly.

	5	5	3	2	2	2
5						
4						
3						
2						
3						
2						

A container can be left empty, part-filled, or filled completely.

A container must have the same level of food everywhere across its width, and all containers must be filled starting from the bottom.

The numbers on the top and left show how many squares are filled in each row or column.

62

Photo finish

Work out in which order these horses finished their race.

The horse in first place has a prime number.

Horse 1 came after horse 2 but one place ahead of horse 3.

Horse 4 finished two places behind horse 1 and three behind horse 5.

Alan Turing's Challenge

What number do you get if you multiply the horse numbers in starting order (1 x 2 x 3 x 4 x 5) and again in finish order, and subtract one from the other?

Twice as ice

Ricky is buying ice creams. He chose strawberry. His sisters want ice creams A and E.

Look at the combinations. Which ice cream is A and which is E?

BC

CD

BE

AD

Alan Turing's Challenge

In 2002, the world's largest sculpture made of ice cream was created at a school in California. But what shape was it? To find out, reverse the alphabet, so A = Z, B = Y and so on.

ZM VRTSGVVMGS XVMGFIB HSRK

City cats

Use the clues to work out which of the cat lovers lives in each city, and what their kitties are called.

Caitlin doesn't own Rocco the cat.

The person in New York owns Silky the cat.

Kendra doesn't live in New York.

The person who owns Clover has a name beginning with the same letter.

Rocco is in London.

Cathy doesn't live in Tokyo.

	New York	Tokyo	London
Kendra			
Cathy			
Caitlin			

	Rocco	Silky	Clover
Kendra			
Cathy			
Caitlin			

Feeling sheepish

Place sheep in all the empty squares so that each row and column has an equal number of white sheep and black sheep.

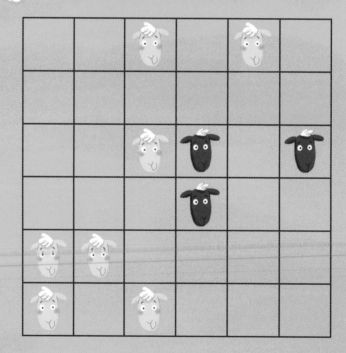

There cannot be more than two black or two white sheep next to each other in a row or column.

Stay hydrated

It's important to drink plenty of water to keep your brain working at its best. In this teaser, which glass will fill up first? Watch out for blocked pipes!

Loads of lemurs

This group of lemurs moved
between the two pictures.
Can you find 10 differences
in the second scene?

Vegetable patch

Divide the allotment into rectangular plots. Each plot contains only one number, which must be the number of dotted squares in the plot. The first one has been done for you.

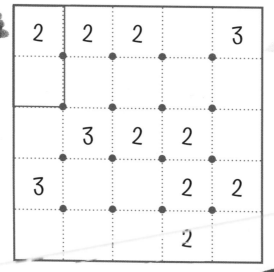

Alan Turing's Challenge

Nancy's carrots are prizewinners at the County Show. They measure 20, 22, 26, 31, and 36 cm. What is their average length?

Who's the champ?

Six children took part in a martial arts competition over the weekend. Work out the order they finished on Saturday, and their final position on Sunday.

Saturday

Zara, Kai, and Sullivan finished in the bottom three.

Mathilde was one place behind Paul.

Lois was in third position and two places above Sullivan.

Kai was not last.

Sunday

Lois moved up two places from her Saturday position.

Mathilde dropped into the bottom three but Kai moved up.

Paul finished below Kai.

Zara climbed a place and Sullivan was one place below her.

Fossil finds

Work out which squares contain fossils for the dino hunter to find. Each number shows how many fossil squares are touching that square (either up, down, across, or diagonally).

Reading time

The librarian has kept a record of which books were borrowed. How many different books were read?

Paco read 7 books.

AJ read 6 books.

Deanna read 5 books.

Two books were read by all three students but there was no other overlap in the books the students read.

Alan Turing's Challenge

If the kids each have to read another new book for homework, and AJ and Deanna choose the same title, how many books have now been read, in total?

Let me in

Nathan needs access to his brother's computer to find some family photos. His brother will only let him on to his laptop if he can work out the 4-digit code. Can you help?

The sum of the 1st two digits equals 12. The 2nd digit is half the 1st.

The last two digits make a square number larger than 40.

The difference between the 3rd and 4th digits is five.

Enter code

__ __ __ __

What 4 digits should Nathan type in?

Alan Turing's Challenge

Nathan's brother changes the final two digits of his passcode. The digits now make a square number larger than 60, with a difference of seven. What code should Nathan type in?

Tuk-tuk teaser

The numbers on this map show the minutes taken for each part of the route. Which of the four tuk-tuks gets its passengers to their destination in the shortest time?

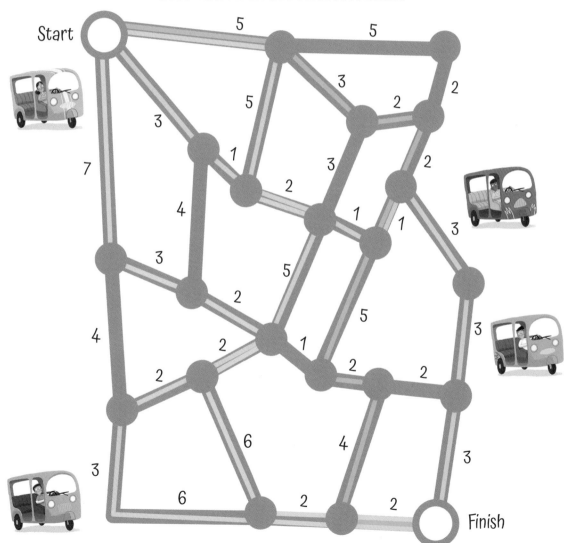

Start

Finish

Moment of truth

Ms. Potts is interviewing four candidates for a job. All four know each other, and may lie to get the job. Which two are liars, and which two can be trusted?

Hint: Do Henri and Paulo's statements match up?

Henri: If Stan is a liar, then Jake can be trusted.

Jake: Neither Paulo nor Henri tells the truth.

Paulo: If (and only if) Jake is dishonest, then Stan is also something of a fibber.

Stan: Paulo's statement is a lie.

Busy lizzies

Which is the only lizard that doesn't share its pattern?

Alan Turing's Challenge

Rearrange these letters to find two types of lizard:

MEHALECON, EOCGK

Genius genie

Find five genies hiding in five lamps. The first one is shown. Use the instructions to work out where the rest are, then make a wish.

There is one lamp in each row, column, and outlined area.

The lamps aren't in squares that touch, even at a corner.

Troll bridge

Help the billy goats cross the bridge without disturbing the troll.

Figure out the missing numbers in the middle columns to match the other columns. Then, choose a path over the bridge to the top only stepping on stones with an even number. You may travel up, down, left, or right, but not diagonally.

Finish

18	22	17	12
5	7	8	4
3	2	?	3
2	?	1	2
8	9	2	3

Start

Alan Turing's Challenge

If the top numbers of the two middle columns were both replaced by 20, would the goats be able to cross?

Shall we dance?

Each side of the diamond dancefloor is made up of three squares in a diagonal line. These three squares add up to the number in the middle. What are the missing numbers?

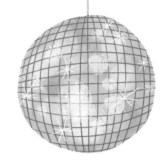

11

4

-1

10

-4

Alan Turing's Challenge

Try it a second time, with a central number of 16.
Do you need any numbers greater than 20?

Sightseeing

Fill in the grids to help you work out who saw each famous sight, and in which month.

The Tanaka family did not travel in June.

The Flynns visited the Statue of Liberty but not in May.

The Santos family saw the Colosseum at the end of summer.

The family that visited the Eiffel Tower went in July.

The Carrolls didn't go to the Sydney Opera House.

	Statue of Liberty	Eiffel Tower	Colosseum	Sydney Opera House		May	June	July	August
Carroll									
Santos									
Tanaka									
Flynn									

Camo close-ups

Camouflage is the fashion this season. But who's wearing what?

Circle where the close-up patterns are found on the models.

A   B   C   D

Zoo-doku

Each of these animals appears once in each row, column, and outlined set of six squares. Copy the animals, or the first letter of each one's name, in the empty squares where they belong.

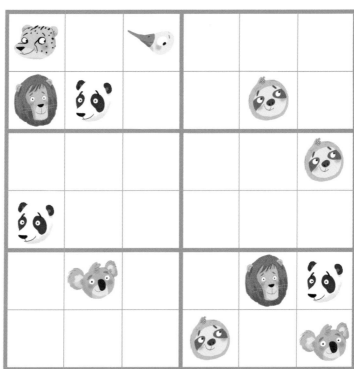

Alan Turing's Challenge

Which three of the animals are found in the wild on the same continent?

Puzzle
SOLUTIONS!

No peeking here until you've given each puzzle your best shot! If you get stuck, try rereading the instructions carefully.

Solutions

Page 4

Add the three numbers around the chip and divide by 2 to get the number on the guacamole dip.

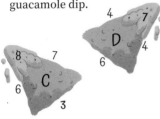

Alan Turing's Challenge

Answer: SALSA

Page 5

3

Each row, column, and diagonal of three frogs has numbers that add up to 15.

Page 6

6 minutes.

Cook two pieces for 2 minutes. Turn one over to cook the other side, and replace one with the uncooked piece. After 2 minutes, take out the cooked piece and turn over the other piece. Put the half-cooked piece back in the pan for 2 more minutes. Now all three pieces are cooked.

Alan Turing's Challenge

10 minutes.

Page 7

Here's one possible solution.

Page 8

Piece 2 fits into pie 1.
Piece 8 fits into pie 2.

Each pie has a difference of 9 between the opposite numbers.

Alan Turing's Challenge

The pieces for each pie add up to the same number.

Page 9

Page 10

Yes, here's how: they can cross in 15 minutes:

Elf Eleanor and Dashing Dwain cross together: 2 minutes.

Eleanor carries the staff back: 1 minute.

Dwarf Dullun and Wizard Will cross together: 8 minutes.

Dwain carries the staff back: 2 minutes.

Eleanor and Dwain cross again: 2 minutes.

$2 + 1 + 8 + 2 + 2 = 15$

Solutions

Page 11

15

Alan Turing's Challenge

Answer: 2

Page 12

3

Alan Turing's Challenge

Answer: 2 and 9

Page 13

The wise woman told them to swap camels, as the <u>owner</u> of the camel that crosses last would win the fortune, not the <u>rider</u>.

Page 14

There are 19 kids in the class.

14 are girls
2 are boys not in blue shirts
3 are boys in blue shirts (8 kids in blue shirts – 5 girls in blue shirts = 3 boys)

Page 15

21

To work it out, add the two paired numbers and multiply your answer by the difference between them, which is 3 each time. So, 2 + 5 = 7, 5 – 2 = 3 and 7 x 3 = 21.

Alan Turing's Challenge

Answer: 6,9. 6 + 9 = 15, 15 x 3 = 45

Page 16

Dale, Clio, Bo, Amy, Eric, Freya.

Page 17

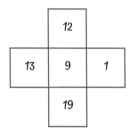

To work it out, replace the letters with their place in the alphabet, so A = 1 BUT rotate them one quarter turn clockwise around the middle value.

Alan Turing's Challenge

Answer: Texas. (The Katy Freeway has 26 lanes of traffic.)

Page 18

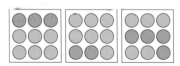

The last set of buttons are all those not pressed in the first two squares.

Alan Turing's Challenge

Answer: 8

Solutions

Page 19

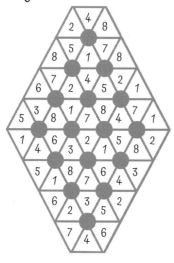

Page 20

The value of the flashing button is 3.

Page 21

40 km/hour.

To work it out: Let's say that one way is 60 km, for argument's sake. So that first journey takes 1 hour.

The return journey takes twice as long. So the total travel time is 1 + 2 = 3 hours.

Their total distance is 2 x 60 km which = 120 km.

Their average speed is 120 km divided by 3, which is 40 km/hour.

Page 22

30

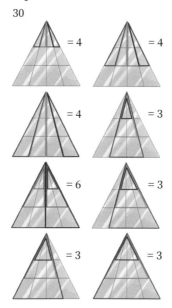

Page 23

K

The horizontal lines stand for a missing letter in alphabetical order, but the vertical lines do not, so K (L), M (N), O.

Alan Turing's Challenge

W L B (Look at the first letters of each word in the instruction...)

Page 24

4 (Even if the first 3 socks don't match, the fourth will always pair up with one he's already holding.)

Solutions

Page 25

	Red Captain	Yellow Captain	Green Captain	Blue Captain
Andy	✗			
Chun		✗		
Frieda			✗	
Joe				✗

	1st	2nd	3rd	4th
		✗		
	✗			
				✗
			✗	

1st		✗	
2nd	✗		
3rd			✗
4th		✗	

Alan Turing's Challenge
27

A 50% increase of 8 is 12, a 50% increase of 12 is 18, a 50% increase of 18 is 27.

Page 26

 = <u>14</u>

 = <u>14</u>

 = <u>8</u>

 = <u>13</u>

 = <u>48</u>

Page 27

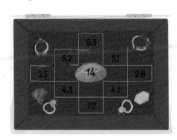

Page 28

120 wrappers divided by 8 = 15.

15 points divided by 5 = 3.

So, the class claimed three medals.

Page 29

C (if you rotate A around the midpoint, you can get to B and D but not C).

Alan Turing's Challenge
Answer: Snakes and Ladders

Page 30

	16	7		
10	9	1	18	
16	7	4	0	5
7	2	4	1	
		13	9	4

Alan Turing's Challenge
Answer: Because the numbers are in alphabetical order.

Solutions

Page 31

They glasses both contain the same proportion of orange and pineapple juice.

To begin, orange juice (O) contains 100 ml and pineapple juice (P) contains 100 ml.

Then Pedro changes it to O = 100 ml O and 25 ml P, while P = 75 ml P.

He removes a quarter of the new mixture (which is 4 parts orange juice and 1 part pineapple so the equivalent of 20 ml of orange juice and 5 ml of pineapple juice) and puts it back into P.

This means that now O = 80 ml O and 20 ml P, while P = 80 ml P and 20 ml O.

Page 32

![]	![]	![]	2
![]	4		![]
2	0		1
![]			
1		1	1

Page 33

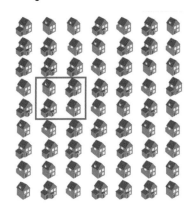

Page 34

Final score
6:05pm

Alan Turing's Challenge

Answer: ARGENTINA. Replace each letter with one 3 letters later in the alphabet.

Page 35

Page 36

Both cars can reach the school with just 2 right-hand turns.

Solutions

Page 37

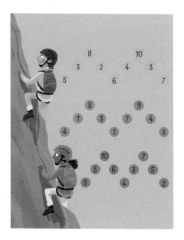

The numbers at the bottom of each "mountain" are the answer to the summit number minus the middle number, e.g. 6 is the difference between 8 and 2, and between 10 and 4.

Page 38

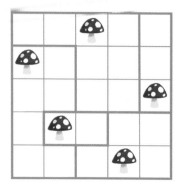

Page 39

301 books (this is the lowest number that is divisible by 7 with none left over. Her previous attempts each have 1 remainder: 300 divided by 2, 3, 4, 5, and 6 each leave 1 book).

Alan Turing's Challenge

Answer: Because page 13 is on the right, with page 14 on its reverse.

Page 40

4. (The numbers on the top tile add up to 10, then 11, then 12, then 13.)

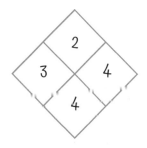

Alan Turing's Challenge
Answer: Guatemala

Page 41

	Basket-ball	Base-ball	Volley-ball	Water Polo
Ben	✓			
Camille				✓
Delany			✓	
Enrique		✓		

Page 42

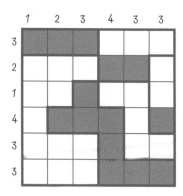

Alan Turing's Challenge
Answer: Less than half: 14/36 (or 7/18)

Solutions

Page 43

It was the Navigator.

One of the Bosun's statements is true, so the thief has to be either the Navigator or the First Mate.

One of the First Mate's statements is true, meaning it must be the Navigator or the Bosun.

The common name between the two is the Navigator.

The Cook and the Navigator both name the same people, each stating an untruth for one of them. Taking the Navigator as the culprit, these statements still fit: Cook's false statement blames the First Mate, and the Navigator's false statement blames the Bosun. So, the Navigator is to blame.

Page 44

15 – the three smaller numbers add up to the biggest number in each set.

Page 45

Aldsfjiob33dflaoyWlopusdSOUS9723
Aoisdn90Ushg**12**Pw78d43posynbWO
opus39bmskh70wndb**12**rs9snyUsgh16
Loysw**82**nfvts973dtsUISO29souUSso9
19sweiUT49nsoDET031snse87&sidP9
dus8%7wd02HDsienUsg238pWs29fn
8sifAl62ndhHH3r9tisl89^3**12**0bsoeOF
$sad93Usgh**12**pW11sbeuBE05*esW5
Pwdb06NBwohgy773&sldi98PPdh56
2&ijWEn85idBRose&£lsib3574iiwi8E

Alan Turing's Challenge

Answer: 4 (in bold, above).

Page 46

He spent 81,660kr in total.

18,000 (taxi) + 1,410 (buses) + 27,000 (hotel) + 9,000 (pass) + 2,250 (Blue Lagoon) + 24,000 (food).

Alan Turing's Challenge

Answer: A 1,000 note, 4 x 100 notes, 2 x 10s and a 5.

Page 47

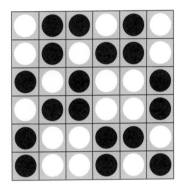

Page 48

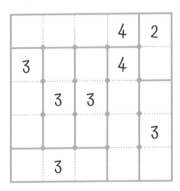

Solutions

Page 49

A = 5 (the difference between the outside ring and inside ring is 12).

B = 6 (the pairs of numbers add up to 21).

Alan Turing's Challenge

Answer: 7:15

Page 50

7 (Adam) and 5 (Belinda)

Moving 1 from B to A gives 8 in one box and 4 in the other. Moving 1 from A to B gives 6 in each box.

Page 51

Alan Turing's Challenge

Answer: Unicorns with a green body. There are 7 unicorns with a green body, 4 with a green mane.

Page 52

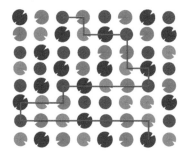

Page 53

8 (numbers in triangles should be added, numbers in squares should be subtracted).

5 + 5 - 3 + 1 = 8.

Alan Turing's Challenge

Answer: 888 + 88 + 8 + 8 + 8 = 1,000.

Page 54

Three shields have no pattern at all.

Page 55

1,071 parts in total (476 wings, 221 engines, and 374 tail fins).

Alan Turing's Challenge

Answer: 110 in five weeks, plus 132 in three weeks, making a total of 242.

Solutions

Page 56

He collects 9 eggs on his route.

Page 57

The monster truck gives the best rate, at $150 per hour.

The yellow sports car costs $156 per hour.

The red off-road jeep costs $160 per hour.

Page 58

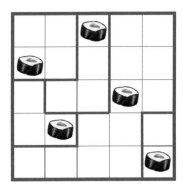

Alan Turing's Challenge
Answer: NIIRGII

Page 59

4 have a green triangle and 2 have a red square.

Page 60

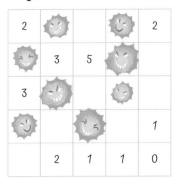

Page 61

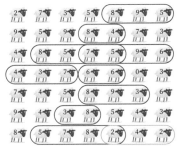

Alan Turing's Challenge
Answer: 11 x 22 = 242, outlined in green.

Page 62

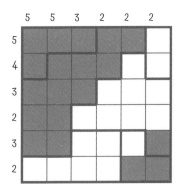

Solutions

Page 63

From first to last to order was 2, 5, 1, 3, 4.

Alan Turing's Challenge

Answer: You get zero, as changing the order for multiplication makes no difference to the answer.

Page 64

A   E

Alan Turing's Challenge

Answer: An eighteenth century ship.

Page 65

	New York	Tokyo	London
Kendra			✓
Cathy	✓		
Caitlin		✓	

	Rocco	Silky	Clover
Kendra	✓		
Cathy		✓	
Caitlin			✓

Page 66

Page 67

Glass 3 will fill up first.

The pipes leading to glasses 5, 6, and 7 are blocked. The water will start to fill glass 3 before it starts to fill glasses 2 and 4. Once the pipe leading out of glass 3 is full, the water will fill glass 3 to the top. This will happen before glass 4 fills completely.

Page 68–69

Solutions

Page 70

2	2	2		3
	3	2	2	
3			2	2
		2		

Alan Turing's Challenge
Answer: 27 cm.

Page 71

Saturday	Sunday
Paul	Lois
Mathilde	Kai
Lois	Paul
Kai	Mathilde
Sullivan	Zara
Zara	Sullivan

Page 72

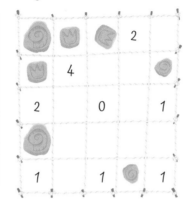

Page 73

14

Alan Turing's Challenge
Answer: 16

Page 74

The code is 8449.

Alan Turing's Challenge
Answer: 8481.

Page 75

Pink takes 26 minutes; Yellow takes 34 minutes; Green takes 17 minutes; Blue takes 24 minutes.

The green tuk-tuk takes the shortest time.

Page 76

Employ Henri or Stan, as Paulo and Jake are lying. (Henri and Paulo can't both be right. If Paulo speaks the truth, then Jake and Stan are trusted or liars which makes 3 liars or trusted–one too many–so Paulo lies, Henri and Stan speak the truth.)

Page 77

Alan Turing's Challenge
Answer: CHAMELEON, GECKO

Page 78

Solutions

Page 79

The first 4 numbers in each column add up to the fifth number. So the ?s are replaced by 4 and 6. That allows the goats to cross safely.

Alan Turing's Challenge

Answer: No, as the ?s would be replaced by 5 and 9, which are odd numbers.

Page 80

	11	
0		4
-1	10	-5
15		19
	-4	

Alan Turing's Challenge

Answer: Yes, you need 21.

	11	
6		4
-1	16	1
21		19
	-4	

Page 81

	Statue of Liberty	Eiffel Tower	Colosseum	Sydney Opera House	May	June	July	August
Carroll	✗	✓	✗	✗	✗	✗	✓	✗
Santos	✗	✗	✓	✗	✗	✗	✗	✓
Tanaka	✗	✗	✗	✓	✓	✗	✗	✗
Flynn	✓	✗	✗	✗	✗	✓	✗	✗

Page 82

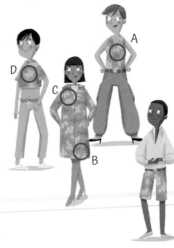

Page 83

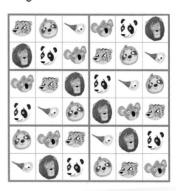

Alan Turing's Challenge

Answer: Lion, ostrich, and cheetah are all found in Africa.